observation is
a constant that
underlies
all approaches

Phyllis Lambert

observation is a constant that underlies all approaches

Lars Müller Publishers

4

6

12

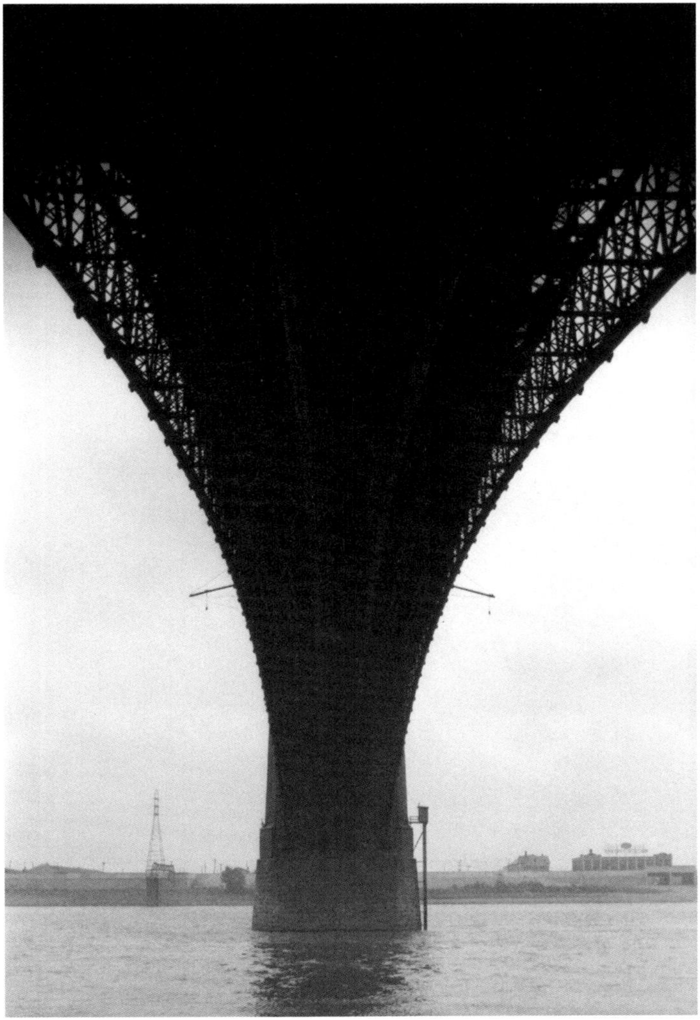

13

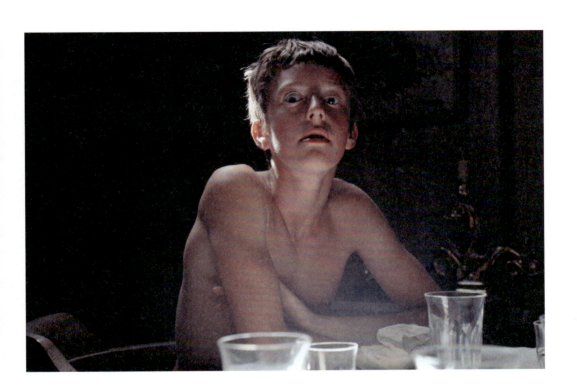

26

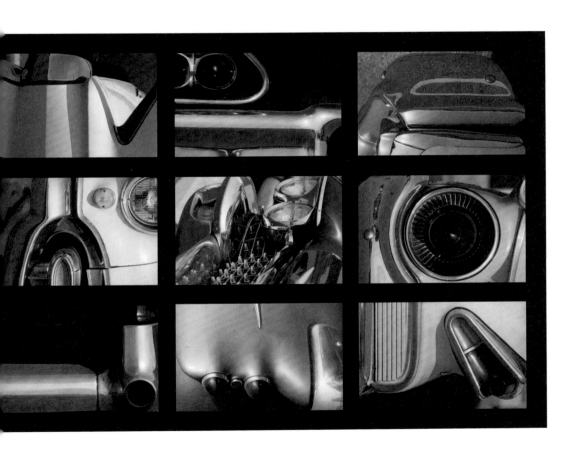

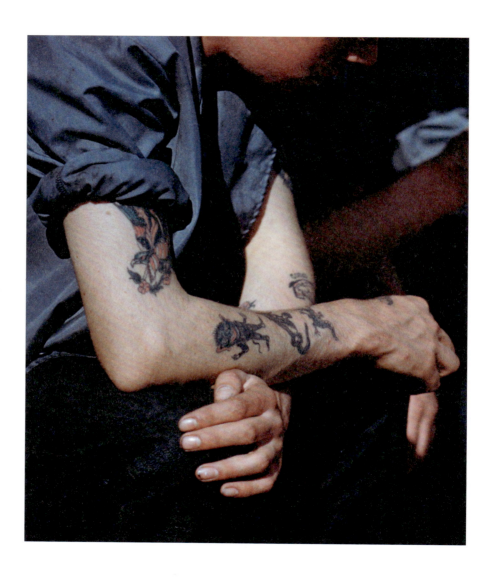

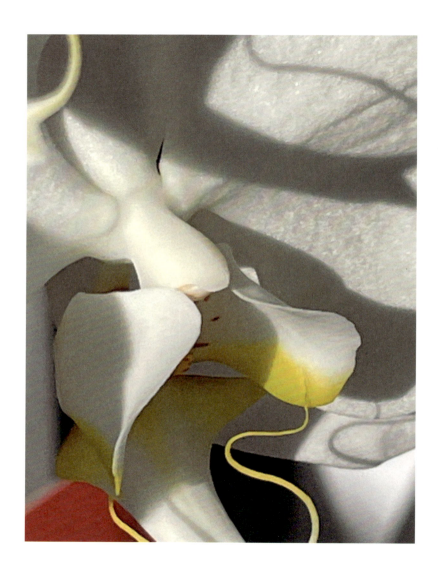

32

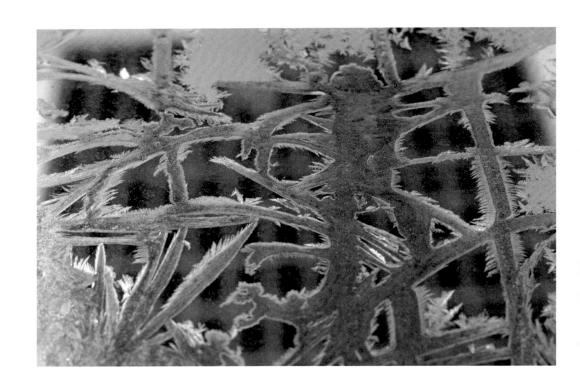

Observation Is a Constant That Underlies All Approaches
Phyllis Lambert

Many persuasive reasons to be involved with photography come to mind. Surely, observation is the constant that underlies all approaches, all levels of interest, and all fascination with the medium. And from observation grows a deepening understanding of the complex interactions between art and the many diverse fields of human knowledge. My own use of the camera dates back to 1954, as I started to think about what a new building in New York – the Seagram building – could be. While in Rome during Easter that year, I began to look more closely at buildings through the lens of a camera I had barely used, observing their qualities, how they sat on the land, their form and articulation, their materials, how architectural details related to a building as a whole, and how the building related to the urban fabric and space of the city.

Four years later, on completion of the Seagram building, for which I acted as director of planning, I went on to train as an architect. I started out at Yale, where I used the camera as part of an assignment in a graphic design course. I continued my professional degree at the Illinois Institute of Technology (IIT), where the lower level of Crown Hall, Mies van der Rohe's great building for architecture, housed the Institute of Design. Aaron Siskind, then a major figure at the Institute, had students working on photographic assignments such as the documentation of Louis Sullivan's buildings in Chicago. Fortunately for me, Myron Goldsmith, my Lieber Meister, invited Aaron to photograph his graduate students' models for a Boeing 727 hangar, among them mine. He became a good friend, one who would ten years later advise me on the Court House photographic project I undertook. But now I am getting ahead of myself.

During that same period, in the context of an IIT course on the history of the city, I developed a keen interest in investigating the palpable, physical manifestations of urban growth. When designing the Saidye Bronfman Centre for the Arts in Montréal, I had begun to see the city I knew with fresh eyes – in particular its strongly defined greystone neighborhoods fanning out from the old city. This became my subject. I asked a young British photographer I knew from the School of the Art Institute of Chicago, Richard Pare, whose clear but poetic work I very much appreciated, to join me in photographing in Montréal during the Christmas and New Year holidays of 1972 and the winter of 1973. Pare worked with a large-format view camera, which was still unusual among young photographers, but I knew it was essential in order to contend with optical distortions such as convergence when photographing buildings. I foraged with my 35mm reflex camera, using a wide-angle lens to map out the greystone neighborhoods that had developed over centuries, and to discover at which time of day the sun best defined the characteristics of the Montréal limestone itself. So began my first photographic mission.

Famously, this undertaking led to the significant decision to return to Montréal and to the rest of my lifelong pursuits – my engagement with the historical, social, and formal aspects of urban planning as new buildings encroached on the old, as well as with collecting the documents of architectural ideation that are the foundation of the Canadian Centre for Architecture, the CCA, in Montréal, with its charge to make architecture a public concern.

What would later become the CCA collection had been initiated in the fifties when I first searched out historical architectural drawings. My curiosity about the kinds of drawings made at other times and in other places was whetted by the studies and drawings made by Mies and members of his office during the process of designing the Seagram building. These "primary source materials" – studies and working drawings – convey the imagined construct of the architect and the process of design. Photographs, on the other hand, register the appearance of buildings, towns, and cities, as well as landscapes, over time, and as such reveal rich urban histories. In response to this sense of purpose in relation to architectural thinking, I acquired in 1974 the first photograph for a collection and an institution not yet created and still only barely conceived of. It was a view of the steps leading up to Santa Maria in Aracoeli on the Capitoline Hill in Rome, with dramatic massing and a real understanding of the way the camera sees, an albumen print from a wet-plate collodion negative made by Robert Macpherson in 1864, acquired from an antiquarian bookseller in New York.

This acquisition, so informally and almost impulsively embarked on, was made at the same time Richard Pare and I were beginning to work on a second photographic mission. For this much larger undertaking in commemoration of the United States Bicentennial, we commissioned twenty-four photographers, most of whom were then little known, to document the American county court house, to study its development across the country. Just as my acquisition of architectural drawings, spurred at first by sheer curiosity, was increasingly fueled by focused inquiry, for the much newer and less understood art of architectural photography, the first order of things was to explore this quickly expanding domain. The moment was decisive: No one could ever put together such a collection today. At that time, hardly any scholarship readily informed the subject of architectural photography. Josef Maria Eder, Beaumont Newhall, and Helmut Gernsheim had written histories of the medium, but there was little else to draw on. We did consult primary sources at the Library of Congress in Washington, D.C., studying the vast Farm Security Administration archive of the photographers who had been commissioned by Roy Stryker to focus on the impoverished lives of sharecroppers and migratory agricultural workers during the Great Depression. By the late seventies, as photographs began to become available at "the fleas" in Paris, in emerging galleries, and at major auction houses, Richard and I brought to collecting an acuity of the eye informed by the art historical canon and by looking through a camera lens, as well as a consciousness of the point of view that stands between the success or failure of interpretation, depth of field, qualities of light, and on both our parts, a rejection of sentimentality.

The photography collection initially formed by Richard Pare and myself points to other avenues for interpreting architecture and the built environment. By default, it demonstrates a view of the medium itself, ranging from the earliest daguerreotypes and salt prints made from paper negatives to the large-scale tableaux and digital prints produced by photographers today. Building a collection of photographs initially representing the first century of the medium required Richard's superb eye, concern for condition, and our mutual engagement with – and openness to – the many different photographic approaches to the built world. From early on, we sought out and chose to emphasize multi-image investigations, from pioneering albums made to be held in the hand to extensive studies of individual structures.

It is interesting for me now to speculate on the extent to which collecting and commissioning photographs influenced my own photography. Perhaps it was Siskind's proclivity for looking closely at things that led me to fall in love with the world seen through the telephoto lens – not with a view camera like Richard and Siskind used, but rather a 100mm lens on a 35mm Nikon camera. I used the still predominant black-and-white film to observe tide pools at the shore, the infinite patterns of wind-blown sand dunes in the Arizona desert, and the fabulous fins and grills of Detroit cars of the sixties in Santa Monica parking lots. I made images that I later combined into photo montages and I became a lens junkie. I was even known to sling a camera over each shoulder, hauling a bag with lenses of various focal lengths as I made the transition from black-and-white film to color slides. I turned to slides because I wanted to transmit to my peers the world of the Aegean – the limpid water, the dry land, the ways land and water meet. I explored the texture of decaying ruins and studied ancient theatres through the camera during summer travels in the mid-sixties while designing the theatre for the Saidye Bronfman

Centre in Montréal, which opened in 1967. The fascination with ancient theatres remained, and later I photographed those at Delphi in Greece and at Pergamon and Aspendos in Turkey, as well as the Roman amphitheatre at Pula in Croatia as a three-slide panorama.

I was also intrigued by processional sequences, disclosing the views that unfold, moment to moment, as one approaches great sites like the dramatically located Greek temple at Sounion. I now realize that, in doing this, I was exercising a cinematographic sensibility learned from Mies's IIT campus, where space flowed between buildings, alternately compressed and expanding, unfolding with the subject's movement down pathways and from one building to another. I made three-screen slide shows coordinated by hand with added sound I had recorded (before it was possible electronically), conveying different cultures of burial in cemeteries from Vermont in the US to the Czech Republic, Turkey, and beyond. That series was extended at Antigua, Guatemala, where volcanos stage the city, and far off in the highlands, portraying the ceremonies of daily life in then still untouched villages such as Chichicastenango in the Department of El Quiché and Trajan's Roman city of Timgad in the Aurès Mountains of Algeria.

During those years, I also created slide shows of threatened Montréal buildings and, using a similar methodology, a TV film for Save Montreal on my return to the city in the early seventies. Among treasured images made during my summer travels and published here are photographs of Justinian's Hagia Sofia in Istanbul, described by the contemporary sixth-century historian

Procopius as "a Church so finely shaped." And indeed it is, in structure, scale, the way the light streams from openings at the base of the dome, and the incredibly rich stone veneers of the narthex and gilded mosaics covering the unfolding vaulted surfaces – the emergence of which I had studied in a seminar led by Richard Krautheimer at the Institute of Fine Arts in New York.

Architectural organizations brought me to many cities internationally where I also photographed, often on the fly. With the members of the International Confederation of Architectural Museums (ICAM), we held tri-annual conferences, first in the Scandinavian countries, starting with Finland, followed by Poland, Russia, Germany, Slovenia, Holland, England, France, and Spain. Some of these I visited numerous times. With the Society of Architectural Historians, I joined a study tour of Russian Orthodox monasteries between St. Petersburg and Moscow, and I took part in another, led by scholars Barry Bergdoll and Dietrich Neumann, to study Mies van der Rohe's early buildings in Berlin while I was preparing the 2001 book and exhibition *Mies in America*. Some photographs in the present volume were taken at the time of the ANY conferences organized by Peter Eisenman and Cynthia Davidson to stimulate dialogue between architecture and general culture on the cusp of the new millennium. These took me to ten cities from 1991 through 2000, some of which I did not know: Tokyo and Yufuin, Barcelona, Rotterdam, Istanbul, and Ankara.

Rarely did I photograph architecture as such. Rather, my interest is in processes, the telling details and the edges around projects I am involved with. In my mind's eye, I remember riding up some thirty stories in an open elevator at Seagram with the construction crew, taking in an astounding view of the raw structure: a field of floor, ceiling, and columns in a penumbra illuminated only by the strip of daylight at the perimeter. Like others, to my regret, the image could not be found. Later, when Seagram was complete, the surrounding buildings and those that replaced them appear in photographs I made of the activity of people on Seagram Plaza, that superlative urban space which met my dreams back then of the social aspects of a city. As architect of the Saidye Bronfman Centre in Montréal, my first commission, I was then involved in every aspect of the project and photographed the construction process in detail – workers in action, tools, cement mixers, huge steel girders stacked on trucks, suction fingers being used to put in place large panes of plate glass, the Mies-inspired seating shell. As I navigated a web of reinforcing rods in heavy construction boots, my camera even led me to observe a circular stair turned the wrong way.

In Cairo, searching for the site that would best represent the co-existence over centuries of the world's three monotheistic religions for an ecumenical center in commemoration of the Camp David Accords, the camera allowed me to study mosques and synagogues and Greek, Catholic, Maronite, and Coptic churches. I decided to focus on the conservation of the Ben Ezra Synagogue and the restoration of its site in Old Cairo, which also includes Coptic churches, other Christian denominations, and, a few paces away, the Mosque of 'Amr, venerated as the oldest surviving mosque in Egypt. Too busy on my tri-monthly visits, I made only a few site photographs, instead asking Richard Pare to capture the completed work as documented in *Fortifications and the Synagogue: The Fortress of Babylon and the Ben Ezra Synagogue, Cairo*, published to ensure that the single remaining synagogue within Old Cairo would be known internationally and thus protected. For the publication *Mies in America*, I asked Guido Guidi and Richard Pare to photograph the IIT campus and the interiors of some of the buildings in addition to the Farnsworth house.

The photographs gathered together here for the first time were taken from the time the camera became a sine qua non of my travels and in connection with my work as an architect, on visits to see friends, and, most recently, for daily observation of my surroundings during the coronavirus pandemic. The medium and instruments varied with each change of time and circumstances. Camera and film, analogue and digital, play a role in the resulting images. Black-and-white versus color was a deliberate choice as well as time-driven. The single-lens reflex camera allowed the use of lenses of various focal lengths. Forcing myself to use a wide-angle or even the standard 50mm lens changed what was observed, and I found alignment was, and still is, the major problem, especially with digital cameras. However, the wide-angle Hasselblad lens captured the delight of the large, crammed, glazed shopfront windows of New York City or the bifurcated symmetrical views where streets and buildings merge. The Polaroid was like the party game Fritz Tugendhat played in the late twenties, providing his guests with photographs of themselves as they left his famous house by Mies in Brno: The secret of instantaneity was a darkroom in the basement. Although I did not abandon the single-lens reflex camera until 1993, by the end of 1986, I decided to reduce the equipment I carried to a camera I could slide into my pocket. Initially, this was an unsophisticated point-and-shoot Olympus camera, replaced in 2003 by the small Canon PowerShot. That it was digital made no impression on me then, but as I look at the prints now, their quality is impressive in tone and gentleness of precision.

Points of view, the fall of light, reflections, and my immediate surroundings were intensified for me with the advent of the iPhone, and a whole new realm of observation opened. Light captured where it barely exists, the fleeting moment fixed, the subjective experience heightened – all became possible with the constant availability of this palm-sized instrument, originally designed to replace the telephone. Here, too, the lens makes a substantial difference. I find it almost impossible to make a dark night view now, for the current iPhone 11 turns night into day, so that one misses those digital images made with the much earlier iPhone 3. These past years of forced isolation during the coronavirus pandemic made the pleasures of observation and experimentation with a subject at close range a daily event. Within the constancy of familiar surroundings, sensual awareness increases. Over more than eight hundred days, I have photographed over and over views from my windows onto the street and the garden terrace, views through the rooms and doorways of the house as light floods the spaces and falls in myriad ways on objects and surfaces. The sun's position and intensity varies the reflections and shadows that abound in all the bodies of work, while night reflections, reflections in reflections, and wind, rain, and snow respond to atmospheric pressure to evoke the subtle changes of seasons. All this takes on the fascination of flickering flames in a fireplace or rolling waves in the ocean. These variations invoke Le Corbusier's observation that "Architecture is the masterful, correct, and magnificent play of volumes brought together in light."

The photographs in this volume, taken with the enormous pleasure of observation through the lens, also recount something about the maturation of a point of view. Richard Pare has expressed such depth with regard to his own work: "The photographer stands before the structure and sees in the stones the rise and fall of the oceans, the rise and fall of empires and fiefdoms, and enters the long centuries where the Roman stones stood abandoned and mute." Observation grows with what it feeds on, driven by focused inquiries that deepen exponentially over time.

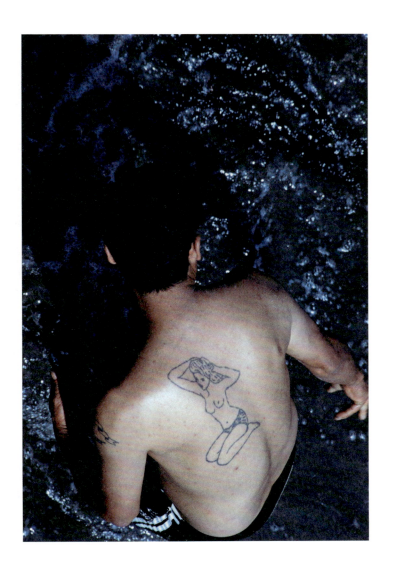

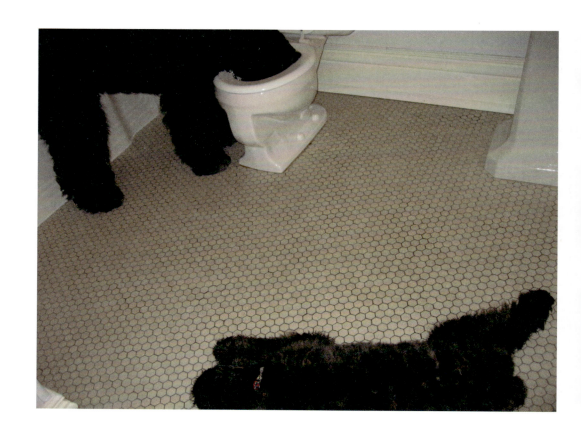

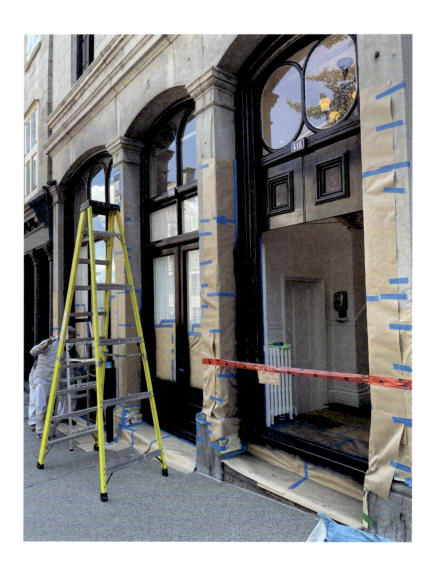

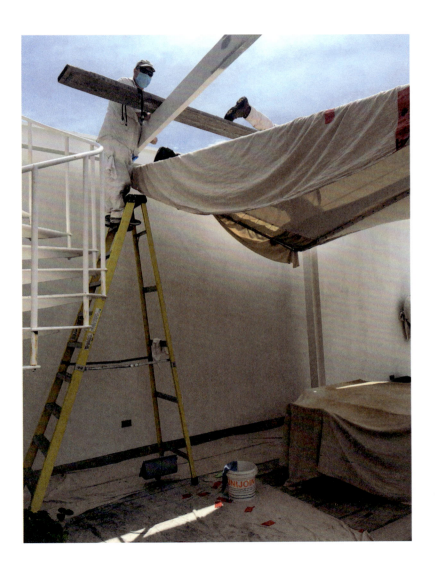

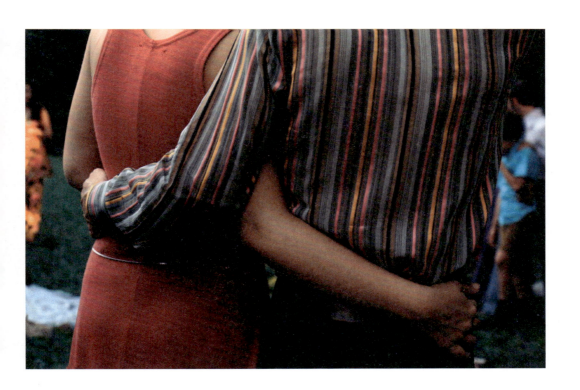

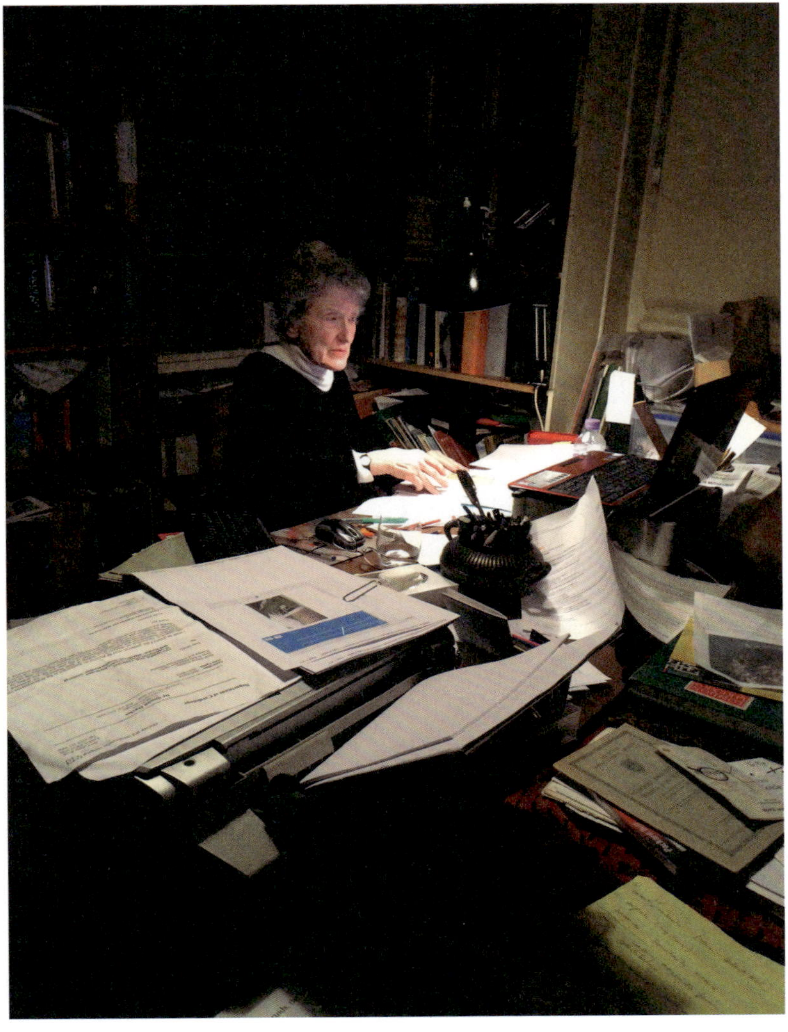

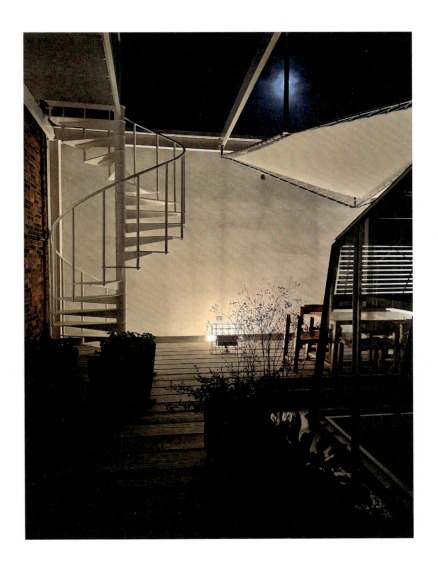

142

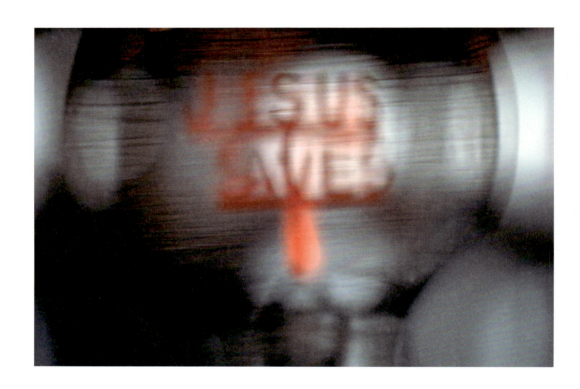

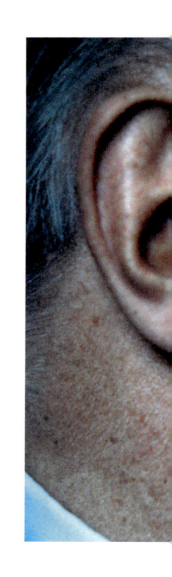

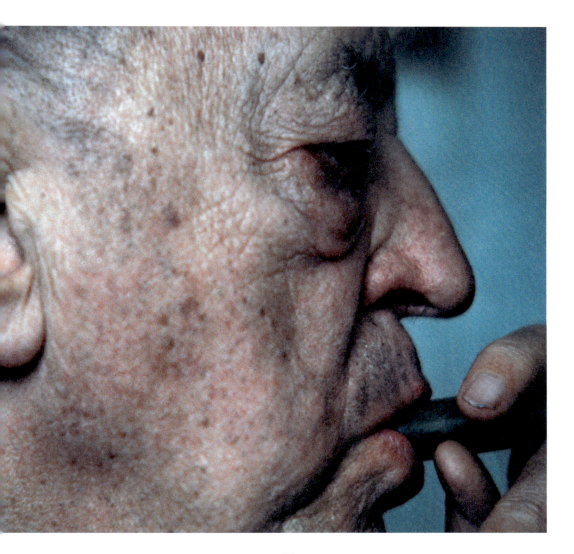

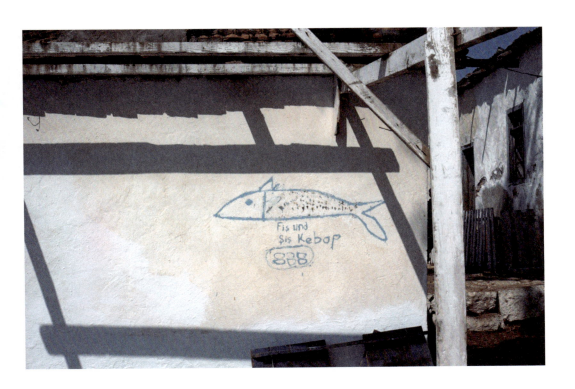

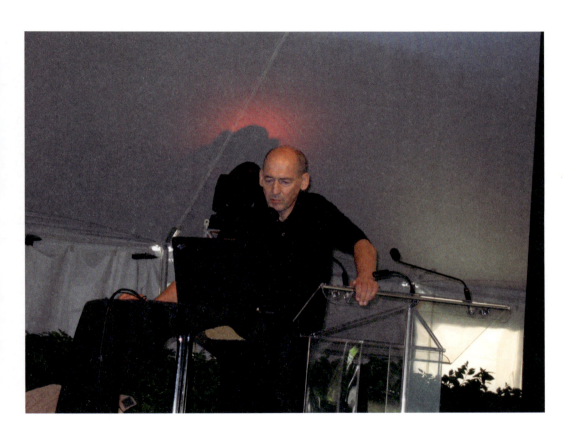

208

232

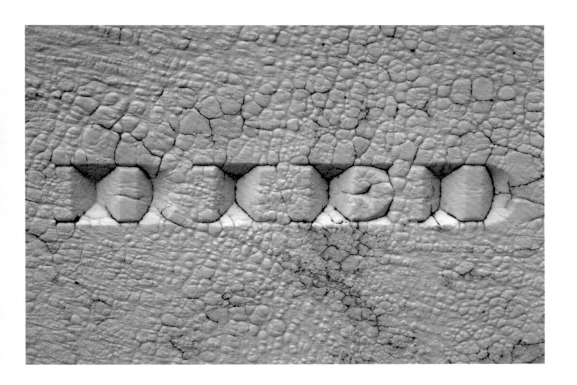

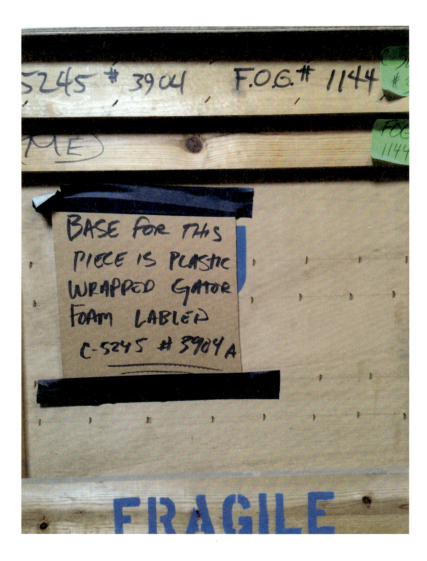

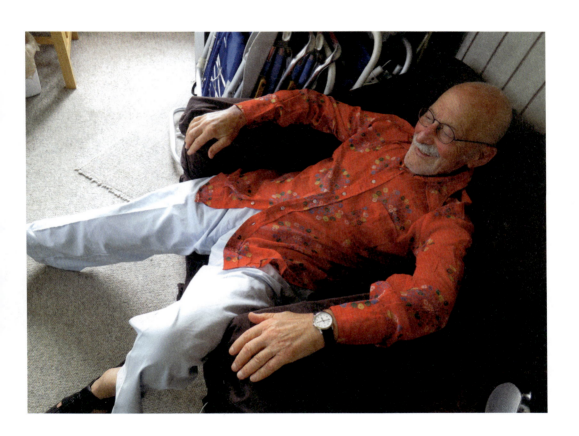

274

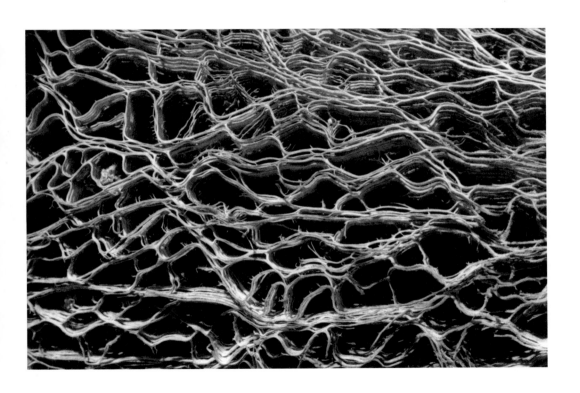

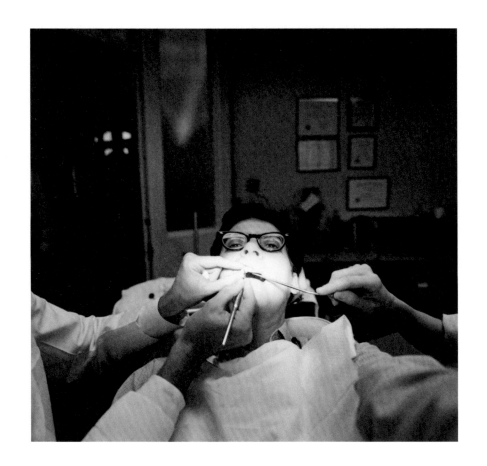

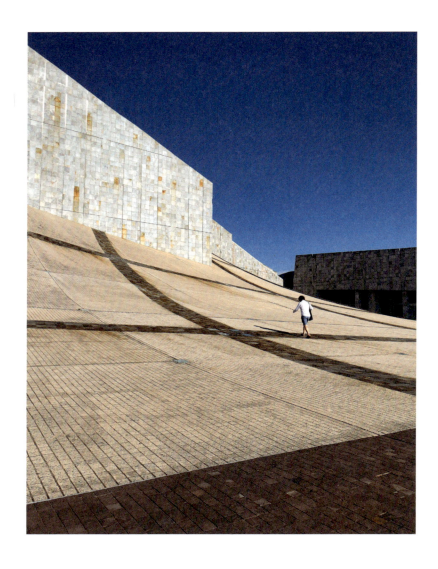

285

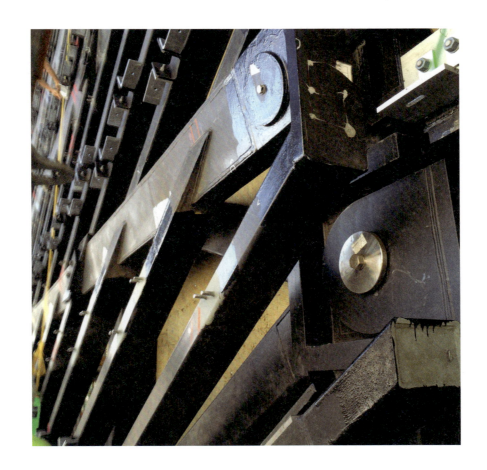

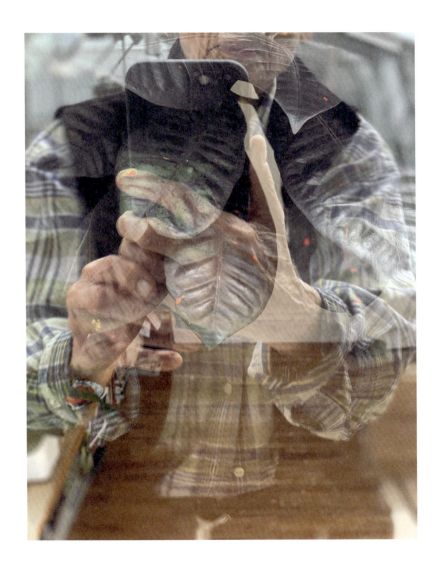

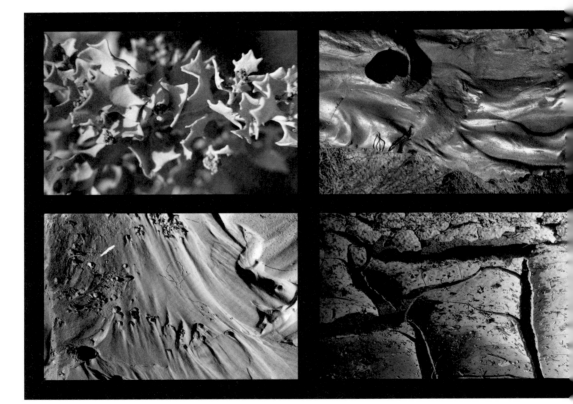

296

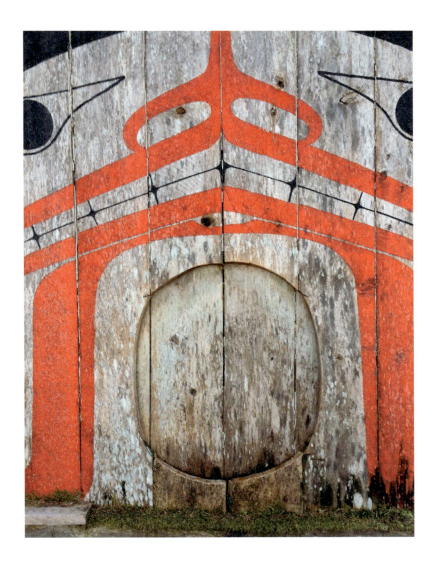

309

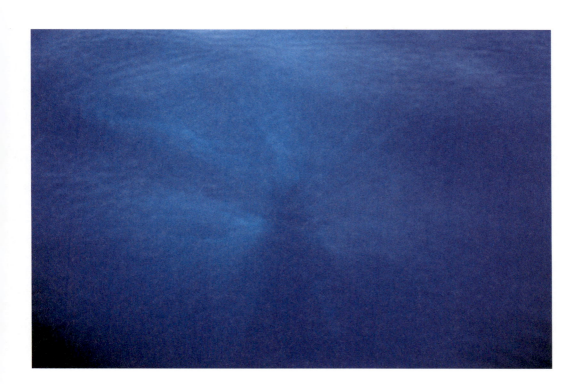

Captions

4 Tribuna, Palazzo Grimani, Venice, Italy, 2013

5 Villa Foscari (La Malcontenta), Oriago di Mira, Veneto, Italy, 2013

6 Rose, Montréal, Québec, 2022

7 Rue Sainte-Famille, Montréal, Québec, 1973

8 Al Giza Desert, Egypt, 1988

9 Alex Tzonis and Liane Lefaivre, Pyramid of Djoser, Saqqara, Giza, Egypt, 1988

10, 11 Jim Dine, *The Plant Becomes a Fan*, at home, Montréal, Québec, 1989

12 Eiffel Tower, Paris, France, 1963

13 Eads Bridge, St. Louis, Missouri, 1963

14, 15 Roman arena, Pula, Croatia, 1977

16 Luža Square, Dubrovnik, Croatia, 1977

17 Street, Yeosu-si, Jeollanam-do, Honam, South Korea, 2013

18 Temple of Hadrian, Ephesus, Turkey, 1983

19 Metropolitan Cathedral, Mexico City, 2005

20 Marble quarry, Paros, Cyclades, Greece, 1968

21 Cologne Cathedral, North Rhine-Westphalia, Germany, 1983

22 Gorgon, ancient necropolis, Finike, Turkey, 1982

23 Flicky eye, 1969

24 Terrace snow removal, at home, Montréal, Québec, 2019

25 Mies van der Rohe, Toronto-Dominion Centre under construction, Toronto, Ontario, 1968

26 Renzo Piano and Richard Rogers, Centre Pompidou, Paris, France, 2018

27 Fondazione Prada, Milan, Italy, 2016

28, 29 Fins and grills, Santa Monica, California, circa 1965

30 London, England, 1961

31 Chinatown, New York City, 2015

32 Phalaenopsis, Montréal, Québec, 2021

33 Garde du corps, Paris, France, 2011

34 Lycian rock tombs, Turkey, 1970

35 Window sill, Rome, Italy, 1978

36 Frost, 860 Lake Shore Drive, Chicago, Illinois, 1971

37 Buckminster Fuller, Climatron, Missouri Botanical Garden, St. Louis, 1963

38 Hagia Sophia, seen from southeast, Istanbul, Turkey, 1982

39 Wooden house, Istanbul, Turkey, 1982

40 Theatre, Myra, Lycia, Turkey, 1982

161 Les Halles, Paris, France, circa 1967

162 Montréal stairs, Anselm-Bissonnette houses, rue Saint-Clément, Quartier Maisonneuve, Québec; photo by Phyllis Lambert and Richard Pare, 1973

163 Domaine des Messieurs-de-Saint-Sulpice, François Vachon de Belmont, towers, 1685; John Ostell, Grand Séminaire de Montréal, 1855-1857; photo by Phyllis Lambert and Richard Pare, 1974

164 Geodesic dome, Haida Gwaii, British Columbia, 2015

165 Friedrichstrasse railway station, Berlin, Germany, 2007

166 Vals, Grisons, Switzerland, 2015

167 Erich Mendelsohn, Einstein Tower, Potsdam, Germany, 2007

168 Onofrio's Fountain, Dubrovnik, Croatia, 1977

169 Relief, Hall of Preserved Harmony, Forbidden City, Beijing, China, 2001

170 Grain distributor, Plum Coulee, Manitoba, 2002

171 Grain elevators, Plum Coulee, Manitoba, 2002

172 Temple of Apollo, Didyma, Turkey, 1969

173 Andrea Palladio, Villa Barbaro Maser, Treviso, Italy, 2013

174 Royal Portal, Chartres Cathedral, France, 1966

175 Rodin exhibition, MoMA Garden, New York City, 1963

176 Autoportrait, 1978

177 Fern, at home, Montréal, Québec, winter 2020

178 Melvin Charney, Column No. 11, Sculpture Garden, CCA, Montréal, Québec, 1989

179 Palast der Republik, Berlin, Germany, 2004

180 Barnett Newman, *Broken Obelisk* with graffiti, Seagram Plaza, New York City, 1967

181 Peter Behrens, AEG Turbine Factory, Berlin, Germany, 2007

182, 183 Mies van der Rohe, Chicago, Illinois, 1964

184 Taj Mahal, Agra, India, 1999

185 Mitla, Oaxaca, Mexico, 2005

186 Cedric Price, 38 Alfred Place, London, England, 1996

187 Arthur Erickson, Helmut Eppich House, West Vancouver, British Columbia, 2002

188 Cemetery, Church of Sainte-Marguerite-de-Blairfindie de l'Acadie, Saint-Jean-sur-Richelieu, Québec, 1977

189 Shish kebab, Turkey, 1982

190 Old Jewish Cemetery, Old Town, Prague, Czech Republic, 1968

191 Burial grounds, Timgad, Algeria, 1965

192 St. John's, Newfoundland, 1977

193 À vendre / For Sale, Westmount, Québec, 1973

194 Gate, Sanssouci Palace, Potsdam, Brandenburg, Germany, 2007

195 Les Halles, Paris, France, circa 1967

196 Corinth Canal, Greece, 1967

197 Richard Pare, Yangtze River, China, 2001

198 Fragments, Delos, Cyclades, Greece, 1973

199 The Great Wall of China, Badaling section, China, 2001

200 Ancient port wall, Monopoli, Apulia, Italy, 2011

201 Unfinished gateway, Villa Trissino Marzotto, Vicenza, Italy, 2013

202 Álvaro Siza, Church of Santa Maria, Marco de Canaveses, Portugal, 2015

203 Álvaro Siza, Hillside Chapel, Praia da Luz, Portugal, 2018

204 Where Álvaro Meets Aldo, Portuguese Pavilion, Architecture Biennale, La Giudecca, Venice, Italy, 2016

205 Rem Koolhaas, CCA, Montréal, Québec, 2007

206 Daniel Libeskind, Jewish Museum under construction, Berlin, Germany, 1997

207 Robert Smith, Jr., Armco-Ferro House, 1933 *Century of Progress International Exposition,* Chicago, moved to Beverly Shores, Indiana, 2003

208 Moshe Safdie, Habitat 67 under construction, Cité-du-Havre, Montréal, Québec, 1967

209 Theatre, Aspendos, Serik, Turkey, 1970

210 Construction site, Saidye Bronfman Centre, Montréal, Québec, 1966

211 Construction site, Saidye Bronfman Centre, Montréal, Québec, 1966

212 Phyllis Lambert, Saidye Bronfman Centre theatre under construction, Montréal, Québec, 1967

213 Phyllis Lambert, Saidye Bronfman Centre theatre under construction, Montréal, Québec, 1967

214 Phyllis Lambert, Saidye Bronfman Centre under construction, Montréal, Québec, 1966

215 Phyllis Lambert, Saidye Bronfman Centre under construction, Montréal, Québec, 1967

216 Construction site, Saidye Bronfman Centre, Montréal, Québec, 1966

217 Barn, Eastern Townships, Québec, circa 1973

218 Norman Wells, Northwest Territories, Canada, 1972

219 House, Olympia, Peloponnese, Greece, 1967

220, 221 Waskaganish, James Bay, Northern Québec, 1972

222 Barry Bergdoll, New York City, 2013

223 Bill Ryall and Barry Bergdoll house, Orient, New York, 2016

224 La Saline Royale, Arc-et-Senans, Doubs, France, 1990

225 Anthony Vidler at Bill Ryall and Barry Bergdoll house, Orient, New York, 2016

290 Baie-Saint Paul, Québec, 2021

291 Autoportrait with plant, at home, Montréal, Québec, April 14, 2021

292 Windshield, Chicago, Illinois, 1969

293 Louis-Philippe Hébert, John Young Monument, Vieux Port, Montréal, Québec, 1978

294, 295 Dunes, Death Valley, California, 1963

296 Faulty Kouros, Apollonas Bay, Naxos, Greece, 1973

297 François Dallegret and Pierre de Wissant, Thorncliffe Park, Toronto, Ontario, 1972

298 Jakob and MacFarlane, Café Georges, Centre Pompidou, Paris, France, 2018

299 Ottoman tombstones, Pergamon, Turkey, 1971

300 Cornelia Oberlander, Vancouver, British Columbia, 2016

301 SGang Gwaay Llanagaay, Haida Gwaii, British Columbia, 2015

302 Wells Coates, Isokon Flats, Camden Borough, London, England, 2005

303 Irena Murray at the Isokon Building, Camden Borough, London, England, 2005

304 Sébastien Le Prestre de Vauban, fortifications, Belle Île, France, 2007

305 Bridge, Chicago River, Chicago, Illinois, 1968

306 Mies van der Rohe, Alumni Hall, IIT, Chicago, Illinois, 2000

307 Laguna Beach, California, 1979

308 Roman bridge, Finike, Turkey, 1970

309 Door, Haida Gwaii, British Columbia, 2015

310 Mosaic floor, Kos, Dodecanese, Greece, 1980

311 Joyce Wieland, Mandraki Harbor, Rhodes, Dodecanese, Greece, 1981

312 Joyce Wieland, Sharon Temple, East Gwillimbury, Ontario, 1990

313 Jean Sutherland Boggs, Sharon Temple, East Gwillimbury, Ontario, 1990

314 Myron Goldsmith, 260 East Chestnut, seen from Mies van der Rohe's 860 Lake Shore Drive, Chicago, Illinois, 1971

315 George Schipporeit, John Heinrich, Lake Point Tower, Chicago, Illinois, 1968

316 Konstantin Melnikov house, Moscow, Russia, 1995

317 Konstantin Melnikov house, Moscow, Russia, 1995

318 Théodore Daoust, Daoust house, rue Saint-Denis, Montréal, Québec, 1975

319 Sheepfold, Kythnos, Cyclades, Greece, 1979

320, 321 Sequence, Temple of Poseidon, Cape Sounion, Greece, 1971

322 Autoportrait, Randolph, Vermont, 1973

323 Autoportrait, Aegean Sea, 1968

Phyllis Lambert

architect, author, photographer, conservation activist, and critic of architecture and urbanism, is the Founding Director Emeritus of the Canadian Centre for Architecture (CCA), which she established in 1979 as an international research center and museum premised on the belief that architecture is a public concern. Lambert inaugurated the field of architectural photography with *Photography and Architecture: 1839–1939* – the first book published by the CCA – and with a series of photographic commissions in the mid-1970s. Phyllis Lambert was awarded the Golden Lion of the 2014 Venice Architecture Biennale.

Acknowledgments

I wish to extend my warmest thanks to the friends who encouraged me
to publish my photographs, and to all those who made this happen:

David Cyrenne, who curated the images and meticulously prepared
the negatives, slides, and digital files for publication. David also undertook
remarkable research to identify numerous sites, as did Adad Hannah
and Katherine Osborne Loigeret.

Glenn Brown, Archivist, Fonds Phyllis Lambert, Canadian Centre for
Architecture, who provided access to the analogue photographs and
participated in their identification.

Photographic Services, Canadian Centre for Architecture

Denise Bratton, Editor

And Lars Müller, who was inspired by the photographs
and shares my convictions.

Phyllis Lambert
observation is a constant that underlies all approaches

Editorial assistance: David Cyrenne
Project coordination: Fanny Rakeseder
Copyediting: Denise Bratton
Proofreading: Jennifer Taylor
Design: Lars Müller with Hanna Welzel
Lithography, printing and binding: Offizin Scheufele, Stuttgart, Germany
Paper: Munken Print White 1.5 vol., 115 gsm

Lars Müller Publishers
Zurich, Switzerland
www.lars-mueller-publishers.com

ISBN 978-3-03778-708-3

Distributed in North America by ARTBOOK | D.A.P.
www.artbook.com

Printed in Germany